Rustle
of Wings

Rustle
of Wings

poems by
Susan Zerner

MIDNIGHT NECTAR PRESS

CALIFORNIA

ISBN 978-0-578-42045-5

Cover art – wings: Sergey Nivens, Shutterstock
Back cover author photo: Stephanie Mohan, Creative Portraiture

Contents

Between my finger
and my thumb
The squat pen rests.
I'll dig with it.

FROM "DIGGING"
BY SEAMUS HEANEY

SINCE I WAS A TEENAGER, my life has been spent trying to uncover who I am, what is the Divine, and how I can connect with it. These poems are some of the reflections of that journey. They are the result of searches to understand darkness, pain, change, death, and to remind myself of joy, possibility, transformation, and connection. An intuitive friend once told me I was like a deep-sea diver, swimming down into the depths of the psyche to bring up pearls. The most luminous pearls have sometimes come from the deepest darkest places.

I didn't grow up thinking of myself as a writer, and my freshman English class in college cured me of any inclination toward poetry. We took poems from Yeats and Keats and dissected them like frogs until all the mystery and wonder was chopped to bits.

It wasn't until I was in my 40's trying out a writing class that something changed. We meditated, then practiced free writing, and I experienced my brain loosening up. I started writing the dream-like images I was seeing which combined unlikely possibilities. At one point the teacher suggested that if I put those free writes into lines, I would have poems. That invitation was the perfect doorway for me to the transformative world of poetry writing.

I wrote most of the poems in this book because there was something difficult I was feeling or trying to understand, a rasping against my heart. Sometimes it can feel like a cacophony of thoughts and emotions swirling around inside me like flies bumping up against closed windows, but I find if I write about it, the windows may open.

Most of the poems are conversations, either between various aspects of myself or between me and my Higher Self/Spirit. They are reflections of the challenging practice to explore discomfort and pain for deeper understanding, even when I'd rather ignore it all or run in the other direction. It is a profound delight when I am able to gather that pain and transform those explorations into poetry.

I have arranged the poems in an arc reading from dark to light (more or less), though, of course, feel free to open the book anywhere; they don't need to be read in order.

The pieces in this book have been gathered over almost 20 years, and I am thrilled and excited to share them. May these words be of benefit to you who reads them.

–Susan Zerner
October 2018

Who was I when I used to
call your name?

FROM "PRAYER"
BY MARIE HOWE

Angel

The angel left a candle burning.
I stare at the flame for courage
amid the massive night.

I look away.
The light blinks out.

I forget where the candle is.
I forget there was a candle.
I forget there are angels.

I think of mystery's hidden teeth
and tremble.

I hear a whisper:

Be still.
Listen with your skin.

You will feel the rustle
of my wings.

A Theory of Holes

Caught
in the jungle of not knowing,
tension ramping up
through the body cavities.

Plug them with fillings
so empty spaces won't ache,
take another hit
of the favored substance to abuse: news,

blues, true things distorted
so reality isn't so hard to swallow—what
is the what of all this, what
is the meaning, what

keeps us careening around,
bumping up against each other
like pin balls all released
at the same time,

the prime directive is
don't feel or reveal
too much of who
you're afraid you are.

There's no end to stuffing the holes
with fake fur though you long
to live in your real skin.

Stop and drop into all those losses,
the places you tossed
aside when you tried to pretend.

You can't vault the chasm
only descend.

Ground in the Change

In the dream an old friend approached me.
She asked how to deal with her crumbling life.

Ground in the change, my dream self said.
When your life splinters into a million pieces
and everything around you collapses on itself,

don't grab at shards as they fly past. Instead,
grieve the firmness of the bedrock you've lost.

Waves of change will hold you just as deeply,
only let yourself be carried.

When I woke up I felt a burst of joy.
And then I thought...
uh-oh.

Scars

Ever seen a grinning little boy
roll up his pant leg
to show off the scabby scar on his knee?
Maybe he has something there.

Adults are too busy
constructing those smooth masks
that cover any lines or lumps
to share scars.

But when you talk to someone long enough,
hidden cracks are revealed:
the 4 miscarriages,
the alcoholic father,
the mother who used her guilt as a stick,

the way the young woman still calls it "non-consensual sex"
because she can't bear to say the R word,
the phone call on a perfectly normal Saturday morning
to say your sister was in a car crash and died.

Everyone has their pain hollows,
tucked in some chamber of the heart
tracing maps of courage.

The Critic

The critic roared up
on his sleek Harley Davidson.
He leaned close, his lips
a heartbeat from my ear. *Putrid!*
he whispered. *Wasteful, clichéd,*
worse yet, fake!

As usual, his words slammed
into my body. Automatically,
my breath locked, stomach recoiled,
shoulders hunched.

Stop it, I hissed sharply,
then realized I was walking through
the lingerie department at Macy's—alone.
Babbling like a lunatic,
said the voice in my head.

The next day, though, as he began
his customary pronouncements,
I noticed a bit of gauze
flapping from underneath
his black leather jacket.

I grabbed the end of it and tugged
hard, unwrapping layer upon layer,
until at last, what remained beneath

was a little girl trembling.
I'm so scared, she said.
I held her close
and sang her to softness.

In the Desert

The sands of my chest are hot,
float like serrated mist.
I am alone.

I keep walking,
but there is nowhere to get to;
my heart is too large
and my will, too small.

The skeleton soul
rattles its bones softly,
urges me to give up,
promises black comfort.

I think I should be able
to bring rain;
I don't know how.
I conjured this desert;
I can't banish it.

The desert says
first you must love me,
be willing to live in me.

Even the vultures
have something
to teach you.

Night

Insect wings flick
against a window
fish dream
with open eyes
crow spies
from the steeple

I gather fear in buckets
it leaks out behind me
through the cracks
in my camouflage
deposits a Rorschach map
in my wake
of intentions gone wrong

I shiver
under dark skies
while cadmium painted berries
wait for birds
who never come
then topple
off their loosened stems

Fear

That lattice of twigs I live on
may soon all topple down.

As leaves spiral to earth,
night will come too and winter,
when frozen roots are hard
and seem forever dead.

Can you be like the leaves,
the darkness asks, and leap,
though you don't know
where you'll land?

I say, but how do I let go?
The darkness answers,

what keeps you holding on?

Nowhere

Mothball-scented closets;
foghorn of a lighthouse barely heard.
A billboard for the diner in 5 miles—
the one boarded up last year.

Fountain of cascading dreams
that never appear in anyone's sleep.
Cash that was lost in the hotel couch
on that last vacation to Miami.

Photo of the smiling couple
in vinyl wallets ready to be sold.
Calypso band playing silent blues.
Sepia secrets under your skin.

Impenetrable darkness with a hidden lock.
Beneath your feet is the key.

What Are Words?

Building blocks of sounds,
plugins for passion or pleasure,
transgressions,
transections of ineffable desires—

what are these strange mouth shapes
that have the power

to let an 8-year-old boy know
he's not alone
when he stands at the empty space
carved from earth that waits
for his mother's body;

or to beguile a teenaged girl
to drag a razor
into her smooth flesh
because all those sneering sounds
have cut her just as sharp.

Sticks and stones only break your bones,
but these bundles of vibrations

can be bludgeons,
blankets, trinkets, visions,

violations, transfusions.
There is magic in these sounds.

We treat the treasures like pennies,
and word by word,
toss away our fortunes.

Nothing to Say

Nothing
batters the inside
of my skin.

Left hand grips
the notebook;

right hand waits
for the pen
to be wise.

I'm afraid
I have nothing to say.

Somehow the nothing
is killing me.

Do You Know What You Ask?

If I told you about this body,
I'd have to feel
the robin curled under my heart
hiding from the rain.
I'd feel the gargoyle
spitting cement in my belly.
Carpets of starlings
looping endlessly behind my eyes.

If I told you about this body,
I'd have to see longings
like old newspapers in the wind.
Burst padlocks of rusted memories.
Regrets fogged and brittle.

But worse, if I told you about this body,
I'd have to hear the whispers
of mothers' mothers and fathers' fathers
back a thousand thousand times,
their tattered souls seared
into every inch of skin.
Unsated cravings of symbiotic ghosts
molding my self.

Don't make me tell you.

Last Moment

I leaned over the cold steel bed rail
to kiss her. I could smell her,
a dark smell
as if her flesh had a head start on decay.

I watched her body
move beneath the sheet with her breath,
each inhale raspy, grating;
each exhale burdened
as she labored toward the last.

What I expected was nothing.
The taxi was waiting
to take me to the airport.

And then, she opened her mottled eyes
and looked at me as if I was just born.
She reached out an unsteady hand
to caress my cheek.

"Ohhhh," she said, her breath barely
carrying the words, "you look so

beautiful." And it wasn't
the words, no,
it was as if her eyes
had opened a conduit to God,
as if I was hit

with a fire hose,
as if all of love
was a sun,
and those eyes
could turn me blind.

This woman who for 90 years
owned such a cramped heart,
at the last moment

shone a light
that was merciless
exposing my own heart's
fortress.

Shell

I always thought it was a metaphor—
that the body is only a shell,
until I saw her still form.

I was afraid to see her,
so my youngest sister, Nancy,
gave a little tug on my arm saying,
"Come on. It's OK."
She held on to me
as we walked together
into the bedroom where my mother
had slept for 53 years.

As I looked down at the bed,
my mother was not there.
All that was left was this hollow structure
with a vague resemblance to who she used to be.
I felt so strongly that if I touched it,
the whole thing would shatter to sand.

Whatever soft squishy sea creature that is the soul
had crawled back into the darkness
leaving this empty carapace behind
and her children to bury it.

Moving Day

I searched in a lightless attic,
stumbling over hatboxes and steamer trunks
my ancestors left behind.

For so long I was a double exposure,
the me I was supposed to be
leaning out from my body,
ghost-like, scrabbling for something.
Never able to touch
the thousand little folds
hiding the marrow.

Grey clouds flow behind the red brick
of the chimney next door.
Nothing will keep those clouds
from sliding.

When all the furniture
waits on the moving van,
the field of nothing
holds me as I sit
on the scuffed wood of the living room floor,
and listen to the echo
of my old selves.

I want to lie down
in the thick of this moment
and feel the pull
on the edges of everything.

Navigation

Your stumbling is a dance.
Each movement
no matter how jagged
fits in the rhythm of the night.

The dung beetle crawls from leaf to leaf
navigating by the Milky Way.
You careen from thought to thought
worried there is no North.

Can't you feel it?
Even when you tumble,
your reeling reveals you—

essential
as the dung beetle
or the whale
or the stars.

Freedom

You have the same staff as Moses
when he parted the Red Sea.

Walk through that damp sandy aisle
littered with old disappointments.

You are more mist than brick,
more wish than certainty,
more dream than deed.

Stop worrying about
what flower you should become

and be with your whole heart
the seed.

Writing Tracks

Here's the problem:
writing is like railroad tracks—

one metal strip carrying
my nebulous bursts of expression,
a parallel strip bearing what's true.

Words are the fragile ties
that try to connect those two.

In the distance
they all seem to merge
in ecstatic communion.

Moon Call

The full moon
is a hole,
a perfect circle

punched through
to the undimmed unknown.

It's the light
leaking
from the universe next door.

Tonight, I stare
through the wind,
my eyes touching
that patient gate,

its full emptiness
plucking
at some abandoned hole
in my belly.

The moon whispers,
come home.

Almost

Just before blossom time,
tight buds recognize
their job is done
and they no longer need
to guard their simmering flower-dreams.

Feel the stirring,
the way each petal still curled tight

is almost ready
to trumpet its yes to the sun,

the way each stamen shivers in impatience,
anticipating its naked offering.

Goddess Soup

I rest in the pocket of her soft frayed apron.
She stirs her tureens full of futures
in the kitchen of time, adding the rosemary,
garlic, carrots and kale.

Then the drops of heartache.
Like lemon juice in soup
you need acidity
to sharpen up the flavors.

I inhale her scent of true Mother
as I drowse in that pocket,
all soft limbs and dark curls.

I know, even with the heartache,
she will not let me fall,
she will not let me fall,
she will not let me fall.

Let Me Dive Deep

Let me dive deep
into that nothingness;
let me skinny dip
in the ocean of void;
let me lie on the bottom
of this great water
and wait,
patient,
hands open.

In the stillness
I am not still.

My breath
dances,
my heart
keeps time,

my cells
divide, join,
are birthed or die,
in ways I
can't ever know.

Silence

Silence tugs
like a single silk thread,

shimmers
like rippling kelp.

Sometimes
it's a mineral bath,

and I dissolve
in its warmth.

Every so often,
the dark honey

is the threshold
to the infinite space

I can't quite remember.

Spirit Tuning

That instant
when a knowing
about myself
falls into place,

like the ringing of a bell,
a crystal sharpness
hangs in the air.

For a moment, I feel
my whole being vibrating
in tune with the universe.

You've felt it too, haven't you?

If every soul opening is a chime,
I wonder if God hears them all as a symphony.

Or maybe after eons,
we're still tuning our instruments,
and the music can't begin

until we learn
how to harmonize.

Lemon Light

Lemon light
poured
through my skin

a quivering peace
in its wake

cooking me into
something more

and something less.

Shifting Contents

All my life when I looked inside myself
there were sharp little boxes of certainty
each one containing a piece of who I thought I was—

either greedy or generous, willful or accommodating,
lazy or industrious, warm or distant.
Only one at a time was allowed.

But yesterday, inside the edges of my skin I saw
the evening sky, no—a galaxy, no—the universe,
not a fixed thing, but a kaleidoscope of fluid parts,
a blur of emptiness and potential.

All the molecules of my body
pivoted a half step deeper and hummed
in tune with everything.

Wedding

For Donna and David

I expected dress, bouquet, vows, kiss, sweet tears.

Instead, when she approached the altar,
the bride stepped into Goddess/Woman/She.
The waiting groom dropped into God/Man/He.
Holding hands, facing rabbi and priest together,
it was as if the energy of each one anchored
in the fiery core of the earth
and shot up in sacred flames to the heavens.

This was no nice couple.
This was the Shechinah and Yahweh.

Two aspects of divinity joined in power.
It reminded me of ancient ceremonies
using humans as stand-ins for gods.

They embodied what a wedding can be—
not just two people coming together to live in tandem,
but the sacred power
of black and white, day and night,
fire and water, earth and air.

The marriage of two wholes
to celebrate the holy whole.

Dancer

Flinging
her ecstasy to the moon,

elongated
in delirious rapture,

the Wild inside her
crackles its skin.

She is the swollen void.

Red Dress

after "What Do Women Want" by Kim Addonizio

I want a red dress.

Not fire engine red
or apple red,

but red like rich wine
rippling inside
smooth clear crystal glass.

Red like lips barely parted,
two inches from my own
just before the sizzle.

I want the red dress to swirl,
hug my churning salsa hips,
carve a clear path

between barely restrained breasts,
so my sweat
knows precisely where to drip.

I want the dress that flashes a signal
to every pair of lingering eyes
that the wearer

is plugged in to the channel

of oh-yeah-baby-just-like-that.
Don't pretend
you don't know which one I mean.
I want that red dress.
Because

I remember now.
That is the dress

of the Goddess.

To My Beloved

I miss you.
I haven't met you yet, but

I miss you.
I feel the whisper of your palm

against my cheek. I remember
the way I have not yet

turned my head into your chest,
nuzzling my nose against your shirt
and breathing in your scent.

We are closing in like magnets—
that final little leap just before they touch.

It's almost time.
I can taste that *almost*
like a murmur,

like the scent of rosemary
lingering on my fingers

when I brush them
over its green stems.

Everything is possible,
even in the gathering dark.

Close your eyes.
Come find me.

Dissolve

There is the rain.
There is the lake.

Cross-legged on the lotus leaf,
I sit still atop the deep clear water,
so pure I can see
brown stripes of the pebbles
resting at the bottom.

Rain falls,
rippling harmonies
over the lake,
the leaf, my skin.

Alive, each drop
wakens me,
then melts my body. Now,
I am the rain, the lake,
rain...lake...
rain...
lake...

Meditation

Wrapped in a shawl of attention,
I was sitting. Still.
Nothing to hear
but the quick confident pulsing of rain against the wood roof.
Shadows of raindrops quivered on my skin
like a tapping on the door to the seed of me.
Then, between one breath and the next,
something inside opened...

Imagine that you've never stood in front of the ocean.
Never seen a picture of the ocean.
Never even heard there was such a thing as an ocean.
But one day, you turned a corner and found yourself
kneeling on the sand
in front of the limitless water
with the majesty of endless waves
and the salty scent and the crashing.

That day, in that tilting moment
it was as if I could feel all the molecules in the universe
had suddenly expanded into their true state;
I could taste the core in each atom
and all the spaces in between.
All creation was filled with volts of sparkling light;
the dust of me diffused into every bit of it.

This Slender Now

On those nights when my heart is beating fast
and I'm afraid I'm going to die, I tell myself, yes,
you are going to die.

Whether I go to the gym four times a week or not,
whether I eat cupcakes or not,
whether I remembered the sunscreen or not,

one morning
I won't be here to wake up again
or go to sleep at night.

Still. I'm not dead now.
I sit on my purple couch
in my own body
I've lived in all these years.

I write about not being dead.
I feel the space of the room,
listen to my pen moving against the paper,
notice the way my left leg crosses my right.

I take a deep breath
and feel joy in how easy it is to breathe,
feel my heart beating faithfully in my chest,

know that my hair and my fingernails

grow so slowly I can't tell,
but I can't stop them even if I wanted to.

I swallow my very own saliva,
and think the thoughts my brain generates
like a perpetual motion machine.

I celebrate this one moment,
nothing special, only arriving
in this slender now.

Acknowledgments

THIS BOOK may be slim, but it couldn't have become real without the help and support of many people.

The biggest thank you goes to all my writing teachers over the years, especially Susanne West, who started me off in poetry; Leslie Kirk Campbell (Ripe Fruit Writing), who taught me so much about the basics and using the senses; Ellen Bass, who is so sharp in her seeing and so kind in her delivery; Kim Rosen, who helped me feel the dream and depth that poetry can hold; Peller Marion, who holds a gentle, supportive, generous space for freewriting; Jane Hirshfield, who taught that 4-day writing retreat the weekend when we were all in shock after the 2016 election, and who invited us to let our writing be weirder; and Marie Howe, fabulous teacher and poet, who wrote my favorite poem about spirituality ("Annunciation"). Extra special thanks to Jane Brunette, extraordinary writing coach, who said just the right thing at just the right time and was a fantastic midwife for this book to come into being.

Thank you to all the teachers for my soul, including Charlotte Kelly and Maria Nemeth, both of whom changed my life for the better in countless ways; Faisal Muqaddam, who has taught me so much about the vast terrain of spirituality;

Deborah Wilder and Lloyde Barde who taught a class that was like a spa for the heart; Elizabeth Seymour, bodyworker, who has a wise heart and wise hands; and Clare McLaughlin, who has been a profound support for my quest to unfold into my best self as well as a cheerleader for my poems.

Thank you to my friends, including my fellow students in Diamond Logos, who are so brave and committed to the journey; Deborah Kelly, who has been a steadfast and supportive friend for 46 years; the Deer Humans Writing Group (Jan, Laura, Wendy, Carol Ann, Candy, Carolyn, and Monnie Reba), who are discerning, thoughtful, and loving; the writers in the Writing from the Heart class who show up with humor and vulnerability; and Susan Kennedy (SARK), who is not only wise, deep, and courageous, but who is also the human embodiment of glitter.

Thank you to my parents who are no longer here and who supported me, even when they didn't understand me. What an enormous gift that has been. Thank you also to my siblings Donna, Sandra, Nancy, and Larry for the deep commitment to continuing our family connections, even when we are all so different. An extra serving of thanks goes to Donna, not only for offering her superb skills to help edit parts of this book, but because it is a fantastic blessing to have a writer/editor as a sibling to share both the challenging parts of the writing journey and its triumphs.

Finally, thanks to you, the reader. Writing the words is only half the circle; your receiving them completes it.